Elegy in a Puddle

poems by

Don Barkin

Finishing Line Press
Georgetown, Kentucky

Elegy in a Puddle

Copyright © 2025 by Don Barkin
ISBN 979-8-89990-117-1 First Edition
All rights reserved under International and Pan-American Copyright Conventions. No part of this book may be reproduced in any manner whatsoever without written permission from the publisher, except in the case of brief quotations embodied in critical articles and reviews.

ACKNOWLEDGMENTS

Some of the poems in this volume appeared in earlier forms in *Houses, That Dark Lake,* and *The Rail Stop at Wassaic,* poetry collections by this author and published by Antrim House Books.

Publisher: Leah Huete de Maines
Editor: Christen Kincaid
Cover Art: Peter Van Dyck
Author Photo: Eve Barkin
Cover Design: Elizabeth Maines McCleavy

Order online: www.finishinglinepress.com
also available on amazon.com

Author inquiries and mail orders:
Finishing Line Press
PO Box 1626
Georgetown, Kentucky 40324
USA

Contents

I Elegy in a Puddle

Elegy in a Puddle 1
Why Old Men Should be Neither Sad nor Happy 2
In Sun and Shade 3
Foolish Tune 4
Aquarium in the Rain 5
After the Blizzard 6
Far Out 7
Someone Peels Out 8
Passing Out at the Hospital 9
From an Upstairs Window 10
As We Age 11
Back Out 12

II Lost in Woods

At the Lake 15
Old Photograph 16
Incident 17
The Death of Socrates 18
After a Rain 19
Lost in Woods 20
Waiting 21
Four Departures 22
At the Cobbler's 23
Sunny and Warmer 24
Travel is Tragic 25
The Tenant 26
In the Old Magazine 27
"We Owe a Cock to Aesculapius" 28
Retirement Benefits 29
The Ignorance of the Ancients 30
To a Graduate 31

III Philosophers Die Young

Philosophers Die Young 35
Need 36
In Orbit 37
A Rainy Fall Day 38
Lifers 39
A Late Raking 40
Stuck in Snow 41
A Common Tongue 42
Men Spend their Days Indoors like Fish 43
A Man in His Statue 44
Dulled Elegy 45

IV Not Who You Thought

Dog and Master 49
Not Who You Thought 50
Elegy for a Good Man 51
After the Memorial 52
Boy and Sock 53
Existence Understood 54
Truly Lost 55
The Docent in his Dotage 56
An Elegy in Stone 57
Boyhood Thanksgiving 58
Weak Elegy 59
A Day at the Beach 60
Who's a Good Boy? 61
The American Wilderness 62
When I Die 63
The Man Who Lost All That Weight 64
The Neighborliness of Light 65
In the Old Woods 66
Death's Progress 67
Flying East 68
A Good Coat 69

V The Old Code of Snow

On Both Sides	73
The Old Code of Snow	74
The Long Way Round	75
Bad Dog	76
The Deaf Are Better Off	77
A Late Walk	78
The Flood	79
A Holiday Note	80
In Winter	81
Prayer at Christmas	82
Surgery at Seventy	83
A Wash	84
The Tyrant Confesses	85
New York to San Juan	86
West to Grand Central	87
Angelic	88
At the Jetty	89
A Sign	90
Calf Song	91
Travel is Travail	92
A Hungry Generation	93
Tragic	94
Ma and Pa on the Pier	95
A Week After the Funeral	96
At the Cabin	97
Light Flows Everywhere	98
Incident in Early Fall	99
Made for It	100
Grammar School	101
A Deer in the Headlights	102
A Pang	103
The Strengthless Arms of the Baggage Handlers	104

For Maggie

though he seemed able at seventeen to have been formulated already by his teen heart. And Victorian? Well, there was a limit — eight in the tradition. But was his thought or the thought?

I. Elegy in a Puddle

Elegy in a Puddle

Because he's gone, he can't see
this inky portrait of a tree,
much less the tree against the sky
which is the limit of the eye,

reminding us that the cost
of Paradise is that it's lost,
while Heaven fitted in a puddle
like a ship is His rebuttal.

Why Old Men Should be Neither Sad nor Happy

Sometimes now I think
of my mother at the sink,
tapping at the pane
if it began to rain,
or sometimes just to wave,
as she can't from her grave.

Though nothing is destroyed
to vanish in the void,
soon my crumbs will leach
down runnels beyond reach
where they'll forget their name
and mine were once the same.

I wish I'd been the kind
of boy who doesn't mind
his mother's smiling gaze
upon him as he plays.
Unless I guessed she knew
one day I'd leave me, too.

In Sun and Shade

In a small town, people are
who they are, no getting away
from what the eighth-grade teacher thinks,
the ex-wife, the hardware guy.
And when the sun at 3 o'clock
passing through this civic prism
dyes the flaking stucco wall
of Magruder's Service Station, the side
by the vacant lot where sharp things rust,
that is where the spirits mingle,
the ones you know or who know you.
And if on foot you stop to gawk
why, there you are among the shades.
Still, the wall can't tell you what you feel
about who you are or wish to be—
the life you've led, the love you've won.
And who knows what Magruder feels,
who sometimes pays to have it painted,
and has himself a wild tattoo
on his upper arm, his wife Leona's
name in flames, for what that's worth?

Foolish Tune

A man is like a goat hung with a bell,
"Here I am," his only news to tell.

A man is like an actor in a play
who never says the things he'd never say.

A man is like the shoes beneath his bed.
Some days he dreams and sends them on ahead.

A man is like his heart stuck on a pole,
a lightning rod for pain its only role.

A man is like his body in a box
untroubled by the wrinkles in his socks.

A man is like the village in his dreams.
It's coming dusk. His whitewashed village gleams.

Aquarium in the Rain

Sensing something like a wall it turned
and wheeled to get a gaping sidelong look
at nothing like the limits it had learned
weaving through the rock-maze of a brook.

"Yet you know neither where you are nor that
you're only swimming mindlessly about,"
the man said in his slicker mooning at
the fish which met his pity with a pout.

Though later he would walk out in the rain
and listening to the drops go pit-a-pat
on his jacket feel a prickling in his brain
like what the fish felt he'd been looking at—

the sense while swimming willfully along
of swerving where a wall would prove you wrong.

After the Blizzard

Out walking on this shrouded day
you try to think these fields were green
the wooden way you try to say
the names of faces long unseen.

And when the sun sat wide and high
and clocks and dusty brooks ran slow,
an aged leaf dropped in to sigh
that fall was on its way, then snow.

Though now the storm has passed and snow
winks like someone in disguise
from a sunny tuft, you know
too soon the world is otherwise.

Far Out

On sultry summer days the fish
that lives in us regrets its wish
to trade a water-world for one
where pants hang damply in the sun.
In Darwin's debt for our ascent
and air as close as in a tent,
we go to where the waves ride in
to hear their oceanic din
recall the life we left behind
but never quite put out of mind.

Like Wilbur Wright forsaking land
for sky we jog across the sand
then plunge beneath the surface lace
into freedom's cool embrace—
and then swim out so far our friends
wonder how such clowning ends,
and whether we'll go dimly down
with fish who never went to town—
or tramp ashore to fish-eyed looks
from strangers surfacing from books.

Someone Peels Out

She'd flung her cigarette
out the window as she tore
past me in her car
with her pedal to the floor,

where it glowed an instant more
although the road was wet
like a fallen star
that hasn't burned up yet.

I guessed a broken heart,
and though she made no sign
her fury made me feel
the fault must be mine.

Hearts that I once broke
shone coldly overhead.
Their light had just arrived
from stars I'd thought long dead.

And now I had to ask
if from across the years
someone had hurled her claim
for loving in arrears.

Passing Out at the Hospital

It was foolish of me to swoon
outside the room where your wife
was going to die soon
and end your natural life.

But she was like my wife,
a hot-blooded hugger and teaser,
and like me you mined your life
for indignities to please her.

I should have had breakfast before
I came to say my goodbyes,
and like her couldn't stand anymore,
and heard singing and closed my eyes.

From an Upstairs Window

The snow shows where I'd been in boots
as maps show old explorers' routes.
I'd dragged a heavy limb out back
which left a pleasant peasant track.
I'd thrown the dog a tennis ball,
and walked to where he let it fall.
And then with wandering steps and slow
I'd dropped my eyes in thought as though
to give my nodding boots their head
while mine went where my musing led—
which if Magellan's maps were good
would bring me back to where I stood.
And like those sailors had to think it's
likely I'd come home with trinkets.

As We Age

She'd rung the bell, but wouldn't come in.
"It's sold." (I knew that bitter grin.)
"At least down there we're near our son—
not the doctor, the other one."

In fall a wind had come to tell her,
Leave the storm-doors in the cellar!
Forsake your maple-shaded street
for a beach that burns your feet.

Now like chattel chained below-decks
who tug at cuffs around their necks,
she grimaces and twists her rings,
then sails away to the edge of things.

Back Out

That angry-sounding drone
was no one on his phone
but a drunk my bike-lamp showed
lurching down the road,

pawing at the air
like a bee-crowned bear.
Yet as I cycled by
something in his eye

made a thudding start
in my rusted heart,
and I felt somehow bound
to wheel my bike around

in order to come close
and get a little dose
and thus inoculate
myself against his fate.

Not that I would like
to get down off my bike
and hear a drunk confess.
And he would like it less.

II. Lost in Woods

At the Lake

Here light once landed like
a fly on a stallion's back,
a flapping honking flock,
the first word God spoke.
Then lengthened like spilled milk,
like a lover on her back.

Now it's a ski-loud lake,
words crumble like stale cake.
To a mind that's walked the plank
itself is what it's like.
And the sky above it blank,
and beneath that sky, your bank.

Old Photograph

The caption says, "The Ghetto at Lodz."
A line of men walk with their sons
who've just been rousted from their cots
by men with growling dogs and guns.

Those stars must mean they're weak of will—
the stars that they themselves sewed on
the coats they wear against the chill
while walking to the train at dawn.

Or maybe just that they'd been taught
to stroll as though in prayer or thought,
those others that one well-aimed shot
will bring malingerers to a trot.

Incident

The next day I saw what it meant
that we'd made a Black man President:

I passed Black people on the street
and didn't look down at my feet.

My wizened neighbor, nodding by,
turned and looked me in the eye.

"When I was ten," he said to me,
"I saw my dad, dressed to a T,

stroll down Main Street like a gent."
A moment—and I saw he meant

(his eyes were white as pearls and wide)
his people had been dignified.

But now I had to drop my eyes
for all who had thought otherwise.

The Death of Socrates

In the last shop on our block
I hung around their paltry stock
of candy on its narrow stand,
each of them the saddest brand,
which my clever friends would mock.

Then paid *Marie* and thanked her for
my powdery chocolate bar—and more.
Now I could wait, a pug-nosed clown
who'd slapped his last illusion down
for what the Heaven had in store.

After a Rain

A yellow leaf had caught a cup
of rain and looked dully up
when a sunbeam caught my eye
to show it to me loping by,
as though on a rain-swept trail
I'd happened on a fairy grail.

Yet if at home I told them, "Elves,"
they'd have to see it for themselves.
Plus praising things beyond your powers
is death to them like pressing flowers.
A forest-haunting ray of sun
had led me to look down for fun

to spoil my day by lighting up
a leaf that elves used as a cup.

Lost in Woods

The footprints in the snow were mine. "Oh, shit,"
which was a word I hardly ever said,
and there was no one else to laugh at it.
Sunset—by morning I'd be numb or dead.

Dusk in woods comes as a thickening
of a thousand things to one, as groping through
a darkened room where every homely thing
has forgotten itself, the room forgets you too.

I walked out onto a road they hadn't plowed.
A man stood on his porch beneath the light
and smoked and heaved the smoke out in a cloud.
Then he went in and shut his front door tight.

A room turned blue behind its scrim of frost—
whatever else he was, he wasn't lost.

Waiting

Waiting for the doctor to be free
the stranded mind scans the mastless sea,
meanwhile wondering what white-coated
sleight-of-hand revives the weak and bloated
beyond that solemn door. The more you wait
the more you dream its magic must be great—

and dream where there is magic that can cure,
a silent world lies leagues beneath the roar
of shuttling time where nurse and doctor stride
through oozy woods remote from wind and tide,
and lit like milk. The nurse stands at the door
and calls you to come in to wait some more,

and you rise up behind her amorously
like a swimmer carried out to sea.

Four Departures

I. Her Freedom

She loves me most when roaring out of town
the leaves take fright and scatter in her wake,
lifting in the air then drifting down
to leave the road more lonely for her sake.

II. Her Freedom

She loves me most when blasting out of town
the leaves take flight and billow in her wake,
then like a shaken bed-sheet flutter down.
She likes to leave things tidy for my sake.

III. Her Freedom

She loves me most when blasting out of town
the shattered leaves swirl down to make me see
the flying tail of a wedding gown
ecstatic at, at last, escaping me.

IV. Their Freedom

She loves me most when roaring out of town
the leaves fly wildly from beneath her car
and leave me gazing with a painted frown,
reminding me that we both go too far.

At the Cobbler's

I like the shoes, these scuffed-up lives
that cram the racks in Tony's shop.
That pair is Pete's who drinks in dives,
and those belong to Blanche the Mop.

And there's a plastic pair as white
as Tommy's daughter's wedding cake,
which he danced shit-faced in that night
and will wear sober at his wake.

I don't see my own so far.
Except to think that pebbled pair,
perhaps a college teacher's, are
what in another life I'd wear.

Old Tony in his crown of smoke
clomps my boots down, his yellow eyes
liking as a private joke
my clueless customer's surprise

at the boots I'd gotten back—
newly soled but mine no doubt:
the leather cracked, the laces slack.
I knew I'd never wear them out.

Sunny and Warmer

While double-deckers rust at anchor,
our dark angels of stone and gravel,
Miguel and Jesus, are laying pavers
at the Bordens' while they travel.

A caftan welcomes television
behind closed curtains, news and weather.
Her son is punishing his drums
in her basement, clad in leather

and deaf to the thrumming of the thruway
buried by a riding mower,
and both outshouted by a Harley,
a weed-whacker, and a leaf-blower.

Car radios quake with wailing women
wronged by men, who's crime's our own,
or gangsters feigning rage in rhymes
insistent as an air-raid drone.

The world is what it is, yet crass
keening broadcast by a car
provokes a royal fury like
a mastodon's embossed in tar.

Travel is Tragic

While the pale-faced classroom clock
sifted hours into drifts,
cartoon countries pranced across
the cracked and lacquered classroom map.
France was grass, and Spain was sand.
China was a thunderhead,
and Africa . . . a sunken wreck.
And thus I clung to my small desk
out past the classroom's sunny swell.

When we set down, the baggage handlers
at De Gaulle must have come
on horse-drawn trams yet smelled of jet.
The next day outside my hotel,
young mothers rushed to work in heels
through gusting showers, the way Miss Milner's
ivory knuckle rapped *Le Rhône*.
From far or near, by inches I
would never stroke that glossy cheek.

The Tenant

Sparks fly upward from the wood
with a crack, then weave and float
and cry in the chimney's dark throat
until they reach the chimney-hood

where letting out their small breath
they put on the gray of death
and go like ghosts into the night—
while just outside the firelight

his face is painted by a spark
that would have warmed him back to life
waiting in the cabined dark
for her to come and be his wife

those weeks ago (now gone to smoke
with his bold scheme to buy the place).
Feeling an icy face
he gives the dying fire a poke

too dull to fetch another stick,
and seeing a slender flame quiver
and give the blackened air a lick,
gives into it with a shiver.

It's not he thinks she's on her way,
he just has nothing else to wish,
as a man in a boat waits for a fish
who has nothing else to do all day.

In the Old Magazine

As blades slap passing swells, his hand swept over
ads for bygone brands of Scotch and watches
its fine subscribers had wanted, or thought they'd wanted,
now all gone like gold-framed family photos
on pianos, old folks gazing with glazed hope
out into the rosy distances of doom.

Those models got old, a distiller's gone out of business,
and that year's sporty coupe is this year's classic.
Only the fine-lined uncommercial columns
still had the aspect of a mind at work,
formed of what once moved across the Deep.
Though now, his age-glazed gaze abob on clauses,
he flipped a page to sigh at that sad skirt
where once he'd plunged beneath the ritzy glitter.

We Owe a Cock to Aesculapius

A man should live just long enough
to settle his debts and bring back the books
charged out on his card. No hospital bill,
no burial bill should slip with a shower
of condolence notes on the sunny rug.

Then begin again, with fury in
his balled-up fists at light like ice,
and glaring with a plumber's squint
through jungled pipes, to find the smiles
in lullabies, the mail in his veins.

Nothing's as sad, the sun gone down,
as an empty garbage can, its lid
on cold cement gaping at
the settled stars. There never was
one streaking star worth weeping for.

Retirement Benefits

Having lost my list of things to do
I thought I'd take my walk, and being shy
when someone passed I'd stoop to tie my shoe.
To flash a sapless smile would be a lie.

Though I don't know what one more lie would hurt.
Life is mainly lying once we're grown—
lies on lies, the way a dog kicks dirt
to hide his shiny prize, a hollow bone

soon clogged and silent as a clotted nib.
Which is why the graveyards seem so dead—
our jawbones are too jammed with muck to fib.
And anything we had to say, we said.

The Ignorance of the Ancients

The dullest Greek would sometimes spot the god's
silver trident sharpening the scud,
and not the nothing we now know was there.

Or hearing willows stirring in the woods,
think, *giggling nymphs* and turning to his wife
survey her face for lineaments of hurt.

So when the medical student meets his corpse,
the aching odor of formaldehyde
means missing someone he will never meet.

And when her phone-call woke you from your nap,
you stared out at the yard and listening hard
found her smile wide among the flowers.

When crashing in with bags, her eyes flamed up
at that ancestral crime a napping man,
you glimpsed the goddess stalking off in pants.

To a Graduate

What advice can I give?
I've never learned the way to live,
while the world still performs for you.
It's May and all your days dawn blue.
At noon you stretch to Heaven in
the twisting sunbeam of your skin.

When I was young I was scared
and hid myself behind a beard.
I kissed no girls and wasn't kissed.
Those years have lifted like a mist
to leave me standing in the clear
with my wife and daughter near.

Clever heads will tell you how,
but was I dreaming then or now?
Dream hands us on to dream
like the reaches of a stream
until we wake. But Dad must keep
his voice down. Children need their sleep.

III Philosophers Die Young

Philosophers Die Young

All day he drew their house—his favorite game.
But later, on the backyard swing he saw
that from behind it didn't look the same.
So now his dandy drawing had a flaw.

He waited like a creature in the shade
of what he couldn't say but only feel,
until the house went back to what God made
before he'd come to wonder what was real.

Now such things don't bother him a bit.
(Though looking down on houses from a jet,
the plunging rooves upend his native wit.)
Plus who is there to tell—and what? And yet.

Need

The way beneath the summer trees
the grass was black until a breeze
raised a bough making way
for a single milky ray
made his mind return to her
and how she always caused a stir—
ever since the day they met
when, he never could forget,
he had frozen like a deer,
not running off or coming near.

Now when her voice grew brisk with will,
he'd dream a voice that would spill
across gray stones and make them glow
like "one whose voice is sweet and low,"
then plant himself beneath a tree,
where she would find him finally
the way a breeze will finally shake
its darkly-brooding dome awake
and lift a limb with sister-force
to let a bright ray run its course.

In Orbit

Though we rocket round the sun
snugly buckled in,
there's something more than fun
in our rollercoaster grin.

Just once I lost my cool,
at a classic-movie talk,
guffawing at some fool
dangling from a clock.

What galactic dread
fed that strangled bark?
That silent star was dead
that dangled in the dark.

A Rainy Fall Day

Though leaves around me fell,
none of them assumed
that it was bound for Hell
or otherwise was doomed.

Uplifted by a breeze
one made a pirouette
as if to show the ease
of life without regret.

It landed on a rock
and was plastered by the rain.
Still it did not take stock,
or press Heaven to explain.

While I went wisely on
as I knew I must
until all hope was gone
of a saving gust.

Lifers

In town they said we'd have to rent a car
or call a cab, but being almost broke
we hitched a ride, then walked, and it was far.
Our ride just smiled like it was a joke.

The payphone where he took our monthly calls
was in a warren of low buildings—wire and brick.
And though we spent the day inside those walls,
when I glimpsed them in the rearview, I felt sick.

The lift that we got back was too polite
to ask us who it was we had inside.
"By now," he drawled, "he's locked up for the night.
He won't be wondering if you got a ride."

Next day my girlfriend left me for a guy
she'd met at work, I couldn't tell you why.

A Late Raking

It's sad to see an old man rake—
sad that he should care
about the difference it would make
to leave a few leaves there.

He won't recall that distant fall
when playing in the park
he thought he heard his mother call
through the dropping dark,

and peddled home pumping hard
until the plunging hill
which would bring him to his yard
where he took a spill

and tumbling landed in
the road and scared a car.
When steep November days begin,
winter isn't far.

Stuck in Snow

You're spinning your wheels! I think I hear her bray
across the frozen lawn. Though we both know
I'd burn the engine out then walk away
before I'd call somebody for a tow.

She shivers in her robe to make me see
that all I've done is prove my cussedness.
But I don't like those arms she folds at me
and her shivering only makes me like them less.

What riles me is she thinks I still have hope—
the way a fool who thinks he's innocent
even when he's hanging from a rope
still kicks against the way his verdict went.

When she gives up and goes inside I'll face
the only jurisdiction in this place.

A Common Tongue

This is the land of bumper stickers—
those brazen boasts and sidelong snickers
made in passing just for fun
as bad boys ring your bell and run.

Once I snagged one from behind
and asked him what he had in mind.
He had the scared and stunted look
of one who'd never read a book.

I'd rather read words that blink
from a stationary page of ink
than fool's gold glinting off of chrome
that you'd never want to follow home.

Men Spend their Days Indoors like Fish

Depressives love the colors of
the linoleum—bad hamburger,
the blue of a harbor by Monet,
and halvah. Nor do the windows here

admit wind. The building is abuzz,
being regional and data-driven.
The flagpole out front is at half-mast
for the soldiers and such. Its rigging chinks.

It is a building, and it has its reasons.
Though a parking garage slouches this way
on a screen somewhere—a kind of temple,
with comings and goings. Its flagpole will clang.

A Man in His Statue

The hero on a horse that makes him sigh
for bravery and doff his solemn hat
turns his son to stone because he's shy.

Every man adores a hero when
with other men he gazes hatless at
a monument to vanished, valiant men

whose lives went by too fast and then too slow
among the other mottled headstones that
wait out their years in shade and sun and snow,

alone except that solemn holiday
when nobody would dare replace his hat
until the sobbing bugle has its say,

and even stone-faced father-figures cry
for boys turned into stone for being shy.

Dulled Elegy

Everything survives,
broken toys and lives,
in a heap that grows
somewhere above the brim . . .
those epic boyhood snows.

My brother's gaze was dim
and strangers shrank from him
as if he were a bear.
I loved him like a brother,
but now he isn't here.

Though dumbstruck like the other
mourners (just our mother
and those two friends of his)
my brother's voice rings clear.
"It's snowing!" And it is.

I recognize your sneer.
The blizzards you hold dear
rage only in your brain.
And the saddest tear
is just as sad as rain.

IV Not Who You Thought

Dog and Master

It's hard to have a dog since he
won't tell you what he wants—maybe
to eat or be let out to pee.
Or else some hunger lost to man
when the vague savannah ran
into the fence where farms began.

He'll wait and then he'll find a pane
of sun to snooze in, and yet not deign
to roll his brown eyes or complain.
Soon like a bubbling brook he'll trot
beside you and not say a lot
except perhaps the day is hot

and you should rest, then jump up
to hunt down he knows what. Good pup!

Not Who You Thought

Strolling down the block my way
came Death herself in a nice green hat.
She smiled but it struck me that
a dead man can not gaze all day
through lacey curtains stitched with bees
at bright green lawns and leafy trees.

Flushing in the slanting sun
like a rock-face turning red,
it dawned on me though he was dead,
my friend had brimmed his days with fun
while I watch the day grow dim
from my seat. Though as for that,

even in a nice green hat
that sunny smile was just for him.

Elegy for a Good Man

His work was teaching kids
the wonders of this world,
which like a colored map
he happily unfurled.

Thus he filled his days
with riches to the brim.
Yet this is not the best
that we can say of him.

I'd thought he was a dog
that neither barked nor bit
but liked a ball or bone—
but no, that was not it.

The rabbis tell a tale
of twelve men on whom rests
mankind's fate and whom
He regularly tests.

The rub is that these men
can't know who they are,
so each of us must act
the part of Heaven's star.

Not by saintliness,
but simply being good
as he practiced his guitar
and built things out of wood.

And now that God has let
him lay his burden down,
we groan under the yoke
which he wore like a crown.

After the Memorial

The tent is gone
that dignified
this raucous lawn.
No groom and bride

began their term
in that trim shade.
A civic worm
where he was laid

a month ago
and knows its trade
goes at it slow.
The men we paid

to pull the stakes
won't come again
when he awakes
in his dark den.

He'll need no tent,
being made
since he went
of sheerest shade,

to stand and hear
the echo of
a widow's tear
let down in love.

The tousled lawn
will have the air
of brooding on
a bright despair.

Boy and Sock

The sock had gotten caught
when his mother shut the drawer.
They said that socks don't feel,
but how could he be sure?

He thought how in the past
whites whipped the dark-skinned men.
They knew it was okay,
or it was okay then.

Sitting on the beach
he'd watch the sea-swells lift
then go down on their knees
bringing him their gift.

So many things are singing
if you only listen,
though only small boys blush
when lifting sea-swells glisten.

He tucked the sock away
without waking his brothers,
and then went back to sleep
among the sleeping others.

Existence Understood

My neighbor just beyond the trees
seems a figure in a frieze
who never steps beyond the wall
where he holds his pose all day
for fear his edifice will fall.

When a neighbor wasn't just a myth,
understand meant *standing with*.
"It's sad," the old jazzmen sigh,
"I never could get with the way
he plays that tune, Lord knows I try."

Existence is at least and most—
a dab of butter touching toast
or the glittering noonday sea
that winks at us but will not stay
and never begs our leave to be.

Truly Lost

A trusted trail had gone to ground
between two shrubs. All I could see
was sunning brush for miles around.

So this was what it was to think
beyond the last emblazoned tree
where leaves like sunny sea-waves wink,

the garden Adam flourished in,
bedecked with fruit. But ominously
stopping there I tasted tin.

I can't recall how I walked out
bloodied at the cheek and knee
though vaguely recollect my doubt

that where the trail had ceased to be,
I'd had a taste of being free.

The Docent in his Dotage

We all agree that *moose* was his best work.
Although the plodding *dog* and planted *cat*
confirm he was a poet, not a clerk.

But now the lanky plumber he calls James
sighs and mumbles, "*Tom*—I'm *Tom*." In time,
only shit and piss will hiss their names.

His cronies croak his name out at the club,
reminding him he never loved them much.
Boo, who bore his kids, still calls him *Bub*.

An Elegy in Stone

When I lie in a box
cradled by great rocks
a glacier pushed aside
(with *gravitas*, not pride),
my friends will take it hard
and raise a marble shard
which weather will efface
then topple from its base
and arrange as rubble
among the weeds and stubble.

I'd rather be a rock
that since it couldn't talk
never told a lie
or made a child cry.
Had rather been a stone
shouldering the throne
of an emperor of ice
that rolled great rocks like dice
and be wakened by the blade
of a garden spade.

Boyhood Thanksgiving

With an hour before dinner to kill
I sat on the back steps and thought
that it could snow—the air was chill
with a wintry scent—and my heart caught

at the thought of a sudden shower of snow
and how the green tousled yard
thinking there still was time to grow
would take being buried hard.

Although I liked the way snow
lay along the black boughs
and made cars go slow
down narrow canyons carved by ploughs.

A few flakes wandered down
while we ate, and that was all—
dusk, and then the sun went down
on the last afternoon of fall.

Weak Elegy

What went on in that head?
Sometimes a breeze blew
lifting a little glitter
as snow resettles a ledge.
He certainly wasn't that girl
sweeping past in an azure frock.
Those firemen in high boots.

Who would he be at the end
when his breezes all lay down
like impalas in the dusk?
They'd say he'd been a thing
and now was something else.
Only, what had gone on in his head?
He'd kept that under his hat.

A Day at the Beach

Behind that grassy swell slept the sea.
But first the burning beach. He shucked his shoes
and, sobbing like a raw recruit, shot free
of his parents' power to coddle and confuse.

That sparkling vasty white-peaked sea
died at the horizon, adults said.
But if he squinted hard, that blur could be
a dazzling sandy beach in France instead.

He hurled himself into the surf to drown,
but failed and groped his way back toward the sun.
Then shunned the mothering sun and dove back down.
Back on the beach, they'd ask if he'd had fun.

Who's a Good Boy?

I had no cause to ask
when he'd brought me the ball
if that's what dogs would call
a pleasure or a task.

Still I faked a throw
just to watch him go
as raucous rivers flow—
for gladness, not for show.

But when he'd sniffed my fraud,
his cocked head said that he
had never doubted me
the way I doubted God.

The American Wilderness

Lift your eyes to see
to the crow's nest of a tree
where the deep sky is the ache
that some men feel in fall,
and crows like shipmates make
their stand against the All.

And the diner's silver man
in tailored slacks and tan
on his stool all afternoon
with a notebook of his bets,
his smile in his spoon,
tea, and cigarettes.

Plus, doesn't it abash
the way a spray of trash
is gladdening the weeds
behind that factory,
as though a breeze blew seeds
where no bright thing should be?

When I Die

My griefs will lift like mist
and join the pale parade
of things that crossed my mind,
a phantom caravan
less fleshy than a worm
guzzled by a wren
in the reign of Charlemagne.

Still, when I overfill
the spaniel's water dish
because I pity him
and it sloshes on the floor,
I moan at mopping up
the damp a great wave makes
stumbling among rocks.

The Man Who Lost All That Weight

The scale like a coiled snake
didn't hiss or blink awake
when he stepped on. How sweet to shake
the heavy burden off of freight
you'd hauled around from state to state

and be a disembodied breeze
skating on the tops of trees
and clearing your old life with ease:
your gaffes in battle and in bed,
plus all the foolish things you said.

Then he awoke and instead
of flying he was in his bed.
And seeing that his dream had fled
felt the sadness Wilbur Wright
felt on having tasted flight.

The Neighborliness of Light

God said, "Let there be the moon and stars."
Then Edison, at his workbench nights,
dreamt of trapping fireflies in jars
and falling stars caught up in trees like kites.

Now in our village, fairy-lights festoon
the huddled houses, church, and shuttered store,
too thickly settled to expect the moon
to silver every sash and eave and door.

And when a big jet on a moonless flight
from L.A. to New York drops blindly down,
the twinkling beacons on the runway might
be streetlights on the road into our town.

Such thoughts like lightbulbs pop on in our head—
but some wait for what dawns on them instead.

In the Old Woods

As long as they're as long as they were tall
summer elms that blotted out the sun
and were lyrical as lightning in fall
lie in state in duff where field mice run.

Having been enamored of the sun
hanging just above them heading west
they'd left the woods behind to be someone,
though now they seem as glad to be at rest.

There's no sorrow in the swallows' homing cry
on finding them laid low and without leaf.
The busy lives of mice and birds deny
these toppled towers their air of Trojan grief.

But that white birch is lengthy as a whale
striking at the sea-swell with its tail.

Death's Progress

We'd always dreamt that when death comes
birds of prey bisect the sun.
But meanwhile, was that kiting kelp
or minnows nipping at our toes?
A nosing shark? A manta ray?
The love-tug of the undertow?

When the shore rose up all sunny,
we heavy-legged it through the shallows,
stalked across the sand to towel
the terror off, then slept and dreamt
of swastikas that sliced the sun.
Woke and went for one last swim.

Flying East

We'd gazed into a canyon of bright rock
so silent that we didn't dare to talk
and wake it from its long-unpeopled past.
Though even the desert sun's daylong blast
had failed to disturb the stony mind
it kept behind its blank gaze like the blind.

And now I dream that I am stone above
towns where men are worried about love
or its waning, work, and that desert bird, cancer.
A sudden updraft cuffs us with its answer
making both my mouth and mind go dry.
The plane falls from Heaven in a sigh,
then heavy as a sofa it sets down
and rolls past lights as friendly as a town.

A Good Coat

I've got a brand-new coat
from the thrift store.
I don't say this to gloat
or cry poor.

But it seems wrong somehow
to benefit
from the sweat of some guy's brow
who'd saved for it.

And I can't believe this coat
was given away
with the owner's vote
worn only a day.

He would have banked on years
of elegance.
Or glimpsed her widow's tears
and scorned expense.

V The Old Code of Snow

On Both Sides

The old know that they're old
and that we find them sad,
as thieves need not be told
that we think they're bad.

There are people we agree
not to understand,
as God once made the sea
standoffish to the land.

Yet waves rise to embrace
the children where they play
who run away then race
arms wide into the spray.

While their elders like dry shells
dream about the roar
of the glassy swells
that carried them ashore.

The Old Code of Snow

The sudden slanting snow was like
a ladder letting down from Heaven.
We'd hankered for that cloudy castle,
left off of all the modern maps
with Hades and the great whales
to break us of our buccaneering.

Now it falls and falls and falls—
a knitted scrim (but bright, not dim).
While into dusk the blinkered buses
travel toward their puddled stalls,
and we pad home in brilliant slippers
to an afternoon before the fire.

At dawn it lies like drear décor,
the wreckage of a splendid dream.
Yet for a spell this inclination,
so long suppressed, to lift our eyes
seemed right as rain, as cows lie down,
as icons roll their eyes toward Heaven.

The Long Way Round

Through the trees at the height
of a bird's nest winked a light
which at sunset I could take
for a hill farm for my sake.
Though what I had been hunting for
was no lamp hung by a door
but at a greater height the spark
a gust uncovers in the dark—
a star not even in a book
where nobody had thought to look.
Anyway, when you roam
it weakens you to think of home.
So on that dusky trail instead
I dreamt about a rented bed
where they might smile but not be bound
to say I'd gone the long way round.

Bad Dog

"I know I gave him plenty," the young vet said,
"but he's *fighting* it." He dragged that leg around
like a branch, then lay his handsome head
sidelong on a grassless patch of ground

and rolled an eye at Heaven, not his master
who'd hollered, "Walk time, boy!" (a ready lie)
and now stood at the edge of the disaster
while he fought like the Devil not to die.

The Deaf Are Better Off

The Parisians who shrug
with marionette regret.
Or Italians whose hands
aim ploughshares at your heart.
The widow's listing head
like a paper straw
bent to every lip.

Or else the leafless elm
that that throws its limbs aloft
entering the sky
like Lee atop his horse,
beside a stunted pine
in its only coat
like Grant without his hat.

A Late Walk

I heard a roar come up on me—
a pickup homeward bound.
Or wind too deep in woods to see
tore saplings from the ground.

Or else it was the Hound of Hell
who's always on the prowl
to hunt down guilty men and tell
the lofty nodding owl.

Now it was silent as the grave
(night put the woods to bed),
I heard no reason to be brave
except my hellbent tread.

The Flood

Where woods had been a lake stood like a dream.
When I stepped in icy water to my thighs

from what I'd teased my "little weeping stream,"
anger blanketed my mind like flies.

I'd have to hike the two miles back, that's all.
Though wading fifty yards would bring me out,

I'm cautious to a fault—crises fall
on me for crimes of hubris and self-doubt.

Now dusk had come to smudge the woods with doubt,
and several times I thought I'd lost the way.

When I woke today, I looked out
at sunlight on those woods which seemed to say

a worried husband with a wild wife
could find himself at the heart of her wild life.

A Holiday Note

It's not wrong to keep a time of year
for sending notes to those whom you hold dear,

not just from habit but because you've found
each counter-note will have a certain sound.

Not like the echo of a village bell
from every farm affirming, *All is well!*

but sobbing geese whose going makes you hear
a *Goodbye!* that once lingered in the air,

like the butterfly that lighted on your rake
you had to wave away for its own sake.

In Winter

The cold is like a wall outside your place,
as white as ice and very near your face.
As tall as everyone you look up to,
the wall stands mute as tall ones always do.

Summer's something else—the heat steals in
and makes itself at home beneath your skin
to glaze your face with misery and salt
until you think your fever is your fault.

The cold is like a sign that says, *Beware,*
the world is hard—you have no business here
where prizes are decided out of sight.
And so you head back in where buttery light

smears a horsehair chair grown smug with fust
and gilds the crumbs of muffins and of dust.

Prayer at Christmas

I can not repay the love
my loved ones freely give.
Then I should lie in bed
in the vilest neighborhood
of this town. Jesus, if it's true
what they say, save this Jew
who loves not the light but the blue
shadows of trees on the snow.

Surgery at Seventy

His worry widens in a gyre
while he counts down each breath.
Is surgery just covering fire
for his assault on death

when he'll look out from a hill
on undefended borders,
and with no one left to kill
wait for further orders?

A Wash

I.

Not Old

Her underpants are pinkish silk,
his socks are thick and gray.
She heaves their laundry in the wash,
spins, and walks away.

Their vivid vestments glint the gloom,
a blazon of young hope,
until their Rose Window lists
like a kaleidoscope.

II.

Not Young

His rugged jeans are wearing thin,
her blouses faded cotton.
She heaves her hamper in the wash
where stained days are forgotten.

She likes to watch his denim twist
around her flowered cotton,
a way to will their cleanly days
will never be forgotten.

The Tyrant Confesses

My father said I wasn't bright
and though he said it out of spite,
I gobbled up the stars and sun
to be the brightest light bar none.

I dragged the cosmos to my chin,
opened wide, and it fell in.
And though my palate glowed with light
my heart was black as anthracite.

Father may have been right once
but now nobody calls me dunce,
I see the Sun God's dying flairs. . .
I'll salt the cosmos with my tears.

New York to San Juan

He saw her off and then went back to work
delivering a monstrous fold-out bed.
It slipped their grip and thundered to the earth.
They shook their heads and cracked their cheeks as though
enchanted to the stone that drags things down.
A sold-out flight outweighs a fold-out couch
yet climbs the sky as lazy as a gull.

He dreamt he was a peasant dazed by faith
who'd consigned his sickly wife to God,
and prayed her plane would dreamily descend
through downy clouds and canopies of heat
that keep the gulls aloft above San Juan,
where wives grow old in wrinkles like the sea
and heavy waves unfold on sloping sand.

West to Grand Central

You could get off where swells are getting on
at dreamt-up places like Noroton Heights,
Green Farms. Their trench coats purr, *I fell
at Belleau Wood.* But they don't look the part.
A squall of boys blows by. To them this is
a forest trail. They'd never plan a day.

Nostalgic for decay, it suits your mood
to lift the shade and moon the backs
of factories and glints of unsung swamps.
The mustached man whose snappy *gendarme's* hat
he wears pushed back stops by to say this train
is headed for that stately dome, *Grand Central* . . .

those pale stenciled stars above; below,
the trench where all ranks gang—their Belleau Wood.

Angelic

The day you realized you'd earned your wings
and that there'd be no annual review
(except the days a stranger smiled at you)
was any day at recess on the swings.

The moment when you knew that you'd been "made,"
and nothing that you'd ever think or do
would make the Maker lose His faith in you,
reminded you of sand and orangeade.

You also thought of what it's finally like
to let your mirror love you as you are—
less like learning how to drive a car
than remembering how to ride a bike.

At the Jetty

His mother would have gulped with fear
to see him on the rocks out there,
but not the hard-faced waves that lurched
past the boulder where he perched.

Since Proteus only saves
His favorites from His waves,
he watched the rollers crest and whiten
and shouted, "*Bow to the God's son, Triton!*"

Today under summer's dome
where boulders slid beneath the foam,
something glittered like a charm.
His Greek beliefs did him no harm.

A Sign

It said the road was closed,
for winter I supposed,
then *Travel at Your Risk.*

Though freezing breezes whisk
a snowy dirt road bare,
I stumbled like a mare.

Those empowered to warn
should tell us when we're born
frankly how things bode,

but that there's just one road
however rough the track—
and no turning back.

Calf Song

The calf was trotting toward its mother
when it broke into a run.
I knew I never have been other
than my loving mother's son.

No one has loved me just for this
(You've had your dram of mother's milk!).
Yet when alone I watch my piss
arcing brilliantly as silk,

I love me as that mother cow
loves her calf—and what is Time
that says since then can not be now
a son must forfeit his sublime?

Travel is Travail

I dreamt my father died
driving to the beach.
In back, I couldn't reach
the wheel though I tried.

They say that life's a *journey*
as though it had a goal.
I think we only roll
from pram to van to gurney

with no one at the wheel
and shaking like a kettle
or like a blowing petal
that thinks the wind is real.

A Hungry Generation

Some kids fell in behind me. I liked their talk
which was mild and slow. Country kids I guessed
must watch less television. Still, when I walk
far out from town I like my own talk best.

Thoreau went to the woods to think things through
away from honest village voices. A brook
carried off the froth of what men knew.
What glimmered at its bottom was his book.

Their buzzing hung around me like a fly
the whole way back to town and our one store
where louder now they crowded in to buy
the chips and soda they'd gone miles for,

then slid away like the stream Thoreau
called Time and never sighed to see it go.

Tragic

Because a spray of crumbs will be my fate,
I left a half-a-sandwich on my plate.

Ma and Pa on the Pier

We saw them on the day they went
watch us sink to sediment,
important once but now no more.

Unclear what they were leaving for,
we made a wry parental fuss
to force them to wave back at us.

When they came home we had no doubt
though altered they would pick us out
from cops and nuns who crowd a pier,

the way Columbus thought it fair
to thank the queen who'd coughed up cash
for a project she thought rash.

A Week After the Funeral

The sun is bright and clouds steer clear of it.
Our neighbor's mower makes a steady moan.
I guess it's only right that we should sit
through this Sunday whiter than a bone.

I read a clotted book and make some notes.
The deck is freshly swept, the lawn is mown.
The minutes knock their hulls like anchored boats,
their gunnels rub together with a groan

reminding us that we are rich in time
(hours till lunch and dinner, and then bed),
and that squandering a Sunday is a crime
against the destitution of the dead,

who just as soon they hadn't ever died.
Finally the sun drives us inside.

At the Cabin

I shot up at the hiss—it was midnight—
and saw like shivering spring flowers the light
of candles blinking in the woods outside,
and then the glint of an ice-skate ride
like chalk across my pond's black slate
rattling each candle on its chipped plate.
As a kid I'd skated at dusk and caught
my blade on branches trapped in the ice—I fought
for balance but was ridden by my weight
down against the pond's hard cheek.
Now a woman's voice called out—I thought
to me until I heard a man speak.
Then they let their skate blades talk instead
like two who whisper fervently in bed.

Light Flows Everywhere

Coffee from a sprawling cup
escapes you while you mop it up.
Sunlight too flows everywhere,
between bright blinds to stripe a chair.

And when somebody throws a switch
and after the accustomed glitch
lights the village Christmas tree,
among the upturned eyes we see

our aged neighbor, blind from birth,
smiling for all she's worth
at glowing lights against the sky,
or rather at our happy sigh,

reminding us what we call light
gleams in crannies out of sight.

Incident in Early Fall

Blondes in heels totter out
on the lawn done up as beams
of afternoon September sun.

While three thin birches at the back
hiss insults with their tisking leaves
("Such flouncy frocks are *wrong* for fall.")

Still, leggy beams that cross lawn
bring tingling beneath the green,
even if their time is short.

Thus a clutch of classy crones
talk trash to no, or weak, effect
on blondes who cross the lawn in fall.

Made for It

Heaven? It wants predicaments
to prove our pluck and common sense.

Whoever made us *sapiens*
and fit the fishes out with fins

that bend the currents to their will
(plus the water-breathing gill)

gave us brows like rippling pools
to separate us from fools

who dream of floating free of friction
and of poetry or fiction

which are our pinnacles of thought,
a rung above a sailor's knot.

So in a furrowed field we see
the triumph of geometry

which bucks us up for any test
until we end as Heaven's guest

where flummoxed by how not to die
we'll make do with knowing why.

Grammar School

"Who belongs to these boots!" the teacher said.
I blushed—my mother would never have been caught dead.
She'd said it with a note of being sure
like country people proud of being poor.

If she'd come home from class without her hat
her mother would have frowned from where she sat
and sent her back to fetch it from the school
without a second thought that she'd been cruel.

Miss Blake was old and fat and frowned at us
who couldn't form a line without a fuss.
But though we pushed in line to get ahead,
she never said our grammar was ill-bred.

And since a teacher never said things wrong,
I heard my father's dryness in her song.
A winter boot is worth more than a boy.
And a girl need not be comely to be coy.

A Deer in the Headlights

When my headlights found the white muff of a deer
lying on her side, I finally got
what Aristotle meant by "pity and fear
at the fall of a greater man," as we were taught,

and had to ask what hope there was for me
when a beast as fleet as snow lay like a log,
whose honest eyes were open wide when she
was walloped by some drunk guy and his dog.

I thought, "A shame, though not a tragedy."
Unless a luckless day of hunting led
to whiskey and his failure to foresee
the death by fate of what he'd wanted dead.

But still no king, and so no tragedy—
just something it was my bad luck to see.

A Pang

All men are drawn to obscurity
and peer into a fish's neuron
seeking pain, or the minor key
of failure in "Martin Van Beuren".

Do fish cry out from their flat brain?
Then suffering belongs to all
and no one need conceal his pain
like a flower in a wall.

Alert Van Beuren rose to fame,
bumbled, and fell so far down
for failure he became a name.
His statue stands in every town.

We wallow in obscurity
and take a guilty lick of dread.
In woods, the horizontal tree,
on shining days the hour of lead.

The "Strengthless Arms" of the Baggage Handlers

Although you have never seen them yourself,
there are places you still suppose to exist.
San Diego, for example,
where the man in the next cubicle
flew his family over Christmas week...
Beautiful weather, a wonderful zoo!
You imagine a sun-splashed elephant
in its glaring enclosure—San Diego.

Not for the Louvre you flew to Paris,
but the baggage handlers who came at dawn
on a grimy tram to stack big bags
in the shadow of the Eiffel Tower
yet would not lift their eyes to it.
Now if you wondered what difference
anything makes, you could go home
and live as a man who has been to France.

Another place you suppose to exist
entered your mind one afternoon
asleep underneath the Sunday papers.
In the Travel Section, in gaudy orange,
was an ancient desert habitation
and a man on his camel. Like you on your couch,
he too will go, when his god wills it so,
to a place even stranger than San Diego.

Don Barkin has published poems in *Poetry, The Virginia Quarterly Review, Prairie Schooner, Poetry Northwest, the North American Review, Harvard Magazine, The Louisville Review,* and other journals. A full-length collection of his poems, *That Dark Lake*, published by Antrim House in 2009, was a finalist for the Connecticut Center for the Book's Poetry Book of the Year award. He has published two other books with Antrim House: *Houses* (2017) and *The Rest Stop at Wassaic* (2020). He has twice been awarded artist grants by the State of Connecticut. Two chapbooks, *The Caretakers* and *The Persistent,* were published by Finishing Line Press.

Barkin was educated at Harvard and Cambridge universities. He is a former newspaper reporter. He has taught writing at Yale, Wesleyan, and Connecticut College. He has also taught high school. He lives in New Haven, Connecticut with his wife, Maggie. They have a daughter, Eve.

www.ingramcontent.com/pod-product-compliance
Lightning Source LLC
Chambersburg PA
CBHW031435150426
43191CB00006B/529